COME IN SEE
WHY WE ENJOY

We Get
Adopted By
McDonalds
With
Judge Gray's
And
Superintendent
Bill's
Help

We are Beech

We eat

We leave

Mrs. Bradley reads with expression

One of the more enjoyable places in school

Physical Education 3 helps keep a body in tune, just as reading, writing, and arithmetic tunes our minds.

MRS. LANE'S THIRD GRADE

Mrs. Kaye Lane

Brooke Anderson

Ernie Anderson

Michael Bromley

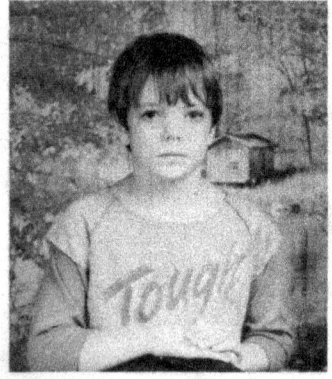

Jeremey Byers

Bryan Caudill

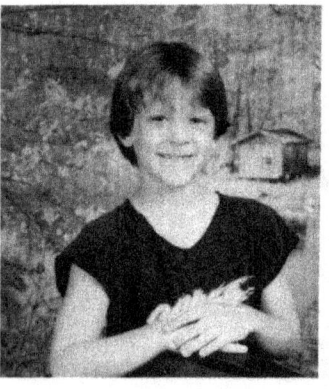

Zac Coppock

Heather Douglas

Becky Elliot

Farrah Fields

Elizabeth Goins

Matt Green

Chrissy Gregory

Shelley Hennessee

Allen Hines

Stacey Holland

Wes Holley

Sabrina Lester

Jamie Matlock

Tommy McClellan

Chris Motley

Cheri Pitzer

Scott Potter

Brandon Ray

Brian Roberts

Matt Robinson

Maria Rose

Ryan Stafford

Bill Thomas

Alison Wicke

Shawn Bowen

Steve Burton

Tamrak Byrne

Triston Carroll

Trey Chrestman

Michelle Cutrell

Michael Davis

Michael R. Davis

Grady Dycus

Nick Holder

Richard Jennings

Carrie Janes

Will Johnson

Michael Kent

Jamie King

Wes Langford

Daniel Meador

Sarah Mickie

Kelley Roberts

Joey Rowe

Kelly Schell

Wendy Scott

Harley Stearnes

Chris Thomas

Stephanie Trew

Sabrina Veach

Margaret Rizor

Matt Wynne

Mrs. Ralph Ann Roach

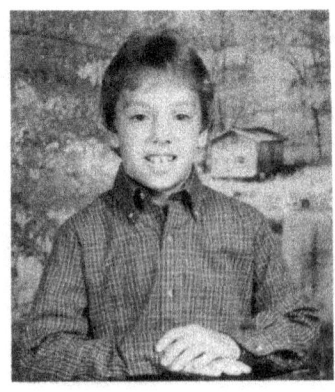

Brandon Austin

Erik Baeder

John Barnhill

Dean Collins

Jaime Cranor

Amber Dancer

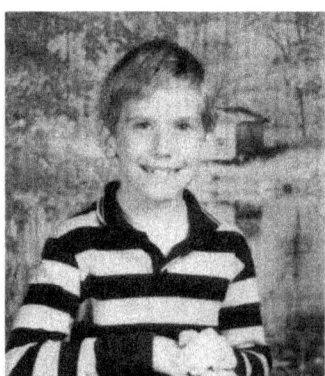

David Dickson

Kevin Earwood

Jason Frakes

David Gilliland

Matt Graves

Philip Graves

Kristi Gray

Leah Gregory

Doug Harris

Michael Hughes

Jeremy King

Curtis Kizer

Stacey McDonald

Brandi Nelson

Eddie Ralph

LeAnne Rusk

Chris Shanks

Mark Vinson

NO
PHOTO
AVAILABLE

Deanna Walden

Brian Webster

Alicia West

Scott Williams

Alisa Young

MRS. BARNETT'S SECOND GRADE

Mrs. Marsha Barnett
Jeremy Arnold
James Baylor
Tiffany Bozarth
James Callahan*

NO
PHOTO
AVAILABLE

Brian Carpenter
Kellie Cooper
Eric Crew
Jennifer Dismukes
Jamie Fultz

Chris Garrison
Trey Graham
Jerry Greer
Airean Jackson
Jeff Kendrick

Ann Kirkpatrick
Brandon Kiser
Jennifer Lomax
Christy Martin
Bethany McKinney

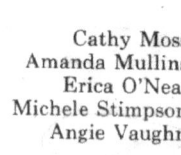

Cathy Moss
Amanda Mullins
Erica O'Neal
Michele Stimpson
Angie Vaughn

Wess Wynne

* Not Pictured

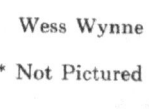

MRS. HOPER'S SECOND GRADE

NO
PHOTO
AVAILABLE

David Adkinson
Richard Bess
Kristen Black
James Brinkley
Billy Burgett*

Josh Davis
Jeremy Fentress
Nicole Fey
Lee Green
Dana Guy

Scott Henry
Beth Lee
Mrs. Melissa Hopper

Becky McBroom
Tommy McMurtry

James McNeil
Shelly Messer
Kori Ann Milkwick
Claire Moore
Julie Owens

Leslie Richardson
Daniel Slate
Joshua Sweeney
Brian Veach

* Not Pictured

Jennifer Bradley
Chad Bridges
Daeg Byrne
Robbie Coleman
Hope Craddock

Jeremy Deloach
Travis Evetts
Robert Floyd
Mike Hannah
Jason Harris

Steven Hines
Korie Hurst
Mrs. Linda Bean

Brandon Kemp
Sam Moore

Michelle Owen
Alexis Page
Edward Qualls
Thomas Rice
Alex Roach

Jimmy Speakman
Heather Strange
Amy Sutton
Jeremy Tomes
Taya Waller

MRS. WILKINSON'S SECOND GRADE

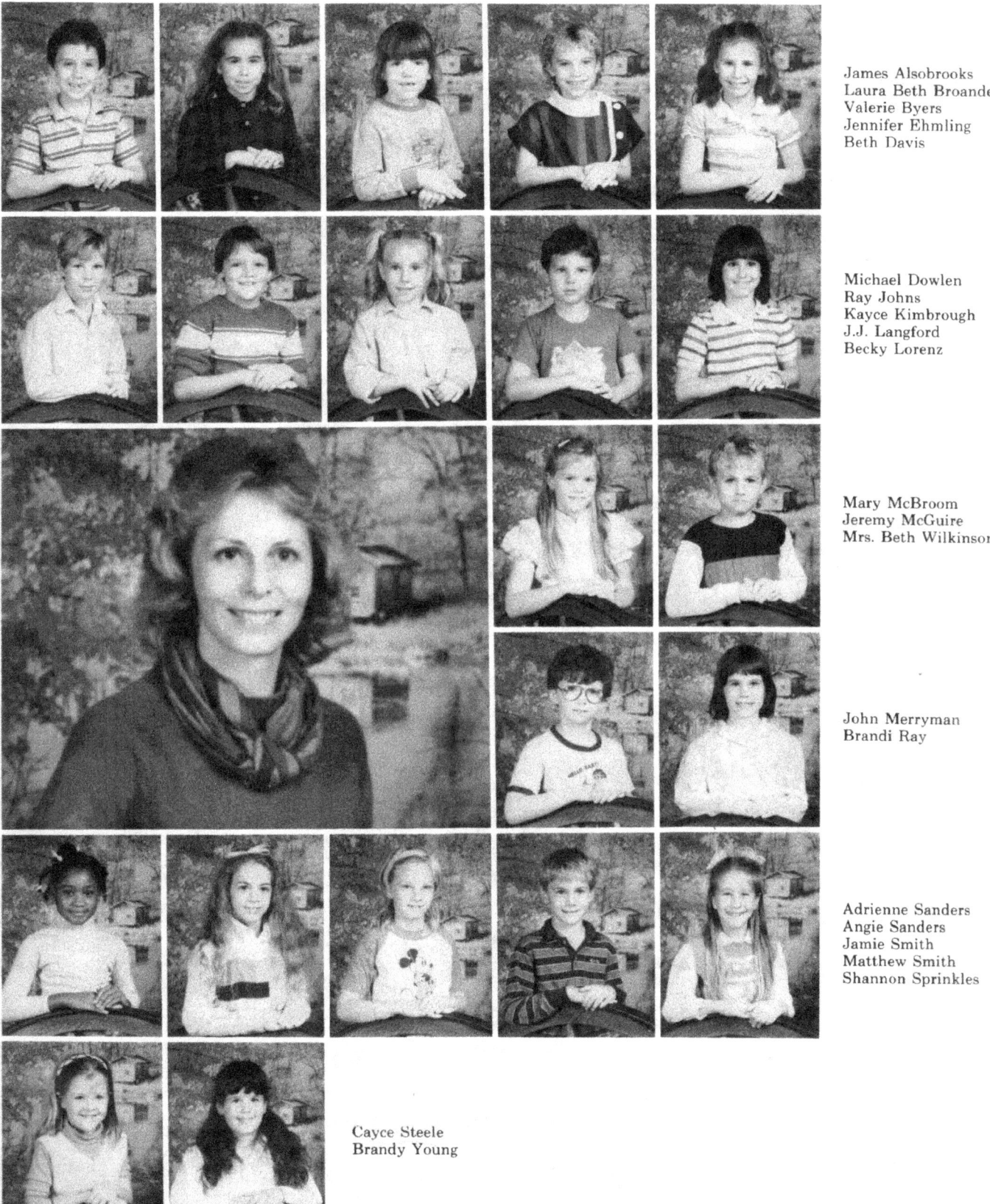

James Alsobrooks
Laura Beth Broander
Valerie Byers
Jennifer Ehmling
Beth Davis

Michael Dowlen
Ray Johns
Kayce Kimbrough
J.J. Langford
Becky Lorenz

Mary McBroom
Jeremy McGuire
Mrs. Beth Wilkinson

John Merryman
Brandi Ray

Adrienne Sanders
Angie Sanders
Jamie Smith
Matthew Smith
Shannon Sprinkles

Cayce Steele
Brandy Young

Mrs. Sheila Jones
Eric Anderson
Mandi Calhoun
Stephen Cope
Lesa Crane

Shellie Crunk
John Dorris
Shaundra Franklin*
Walton Garrison
Jennifer Green*

NO PHOTO AVAILABLE

NO PHOTO AVAILABLE

Joshua Hannah
Terri Lynne Harris
Ryan Hennessee
Lorianne Hines
Carla Hosale

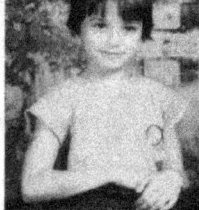  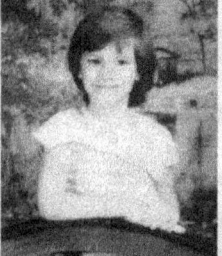 

Carlotta Hosale
Stacey Lawrence
Travis Marlow
Stacy McConnell
Amy Nelson

Brandi Owen
Jonathan Qualls
Crystal Savely
Amber Selph
Kevin Skinner

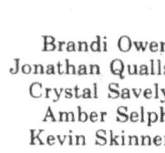     

Blake Southall
Brian Staggs
Brandi Taylor
Andy Young

* Not Pictured

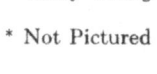   

MRS. HARRISON'S FIRST GRADE

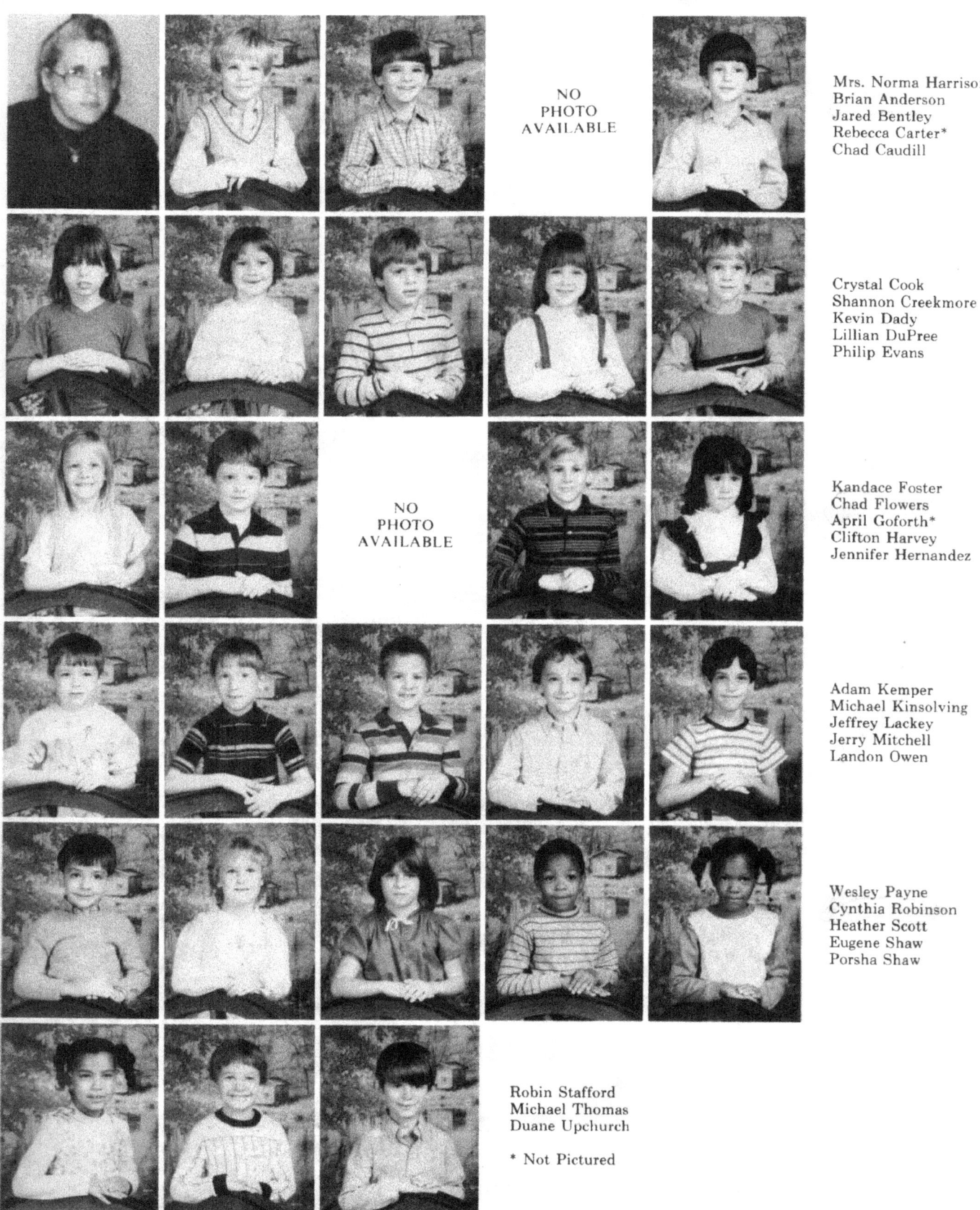

NO PHOTO AVAILABLE

Mrs. Norma Harrison
Brian Anderson
Jared Bentley
Rebecca Carter*
Chad Caudill

Crystal Cook
Shannon Creekmore
Kevin Dady
Lillian DuPree
Philip Evans

NO PHOTO AVAILABLE

Kandace Foster
Chad Flowers
April Goforth*
Clifton Harvey
Jennifer Hernandez

Adam Kemper
Michael Kinsolving
Jeffrey Lackey
Jerry Mitchell
Landon Owen

Wesley Payne
Cynthia Robinson
Heather Scott
Eugene Shaw
Porsha Shaw

Robin Stafford
Michael Thomas
Duane Upchurch

* Not Pictured

Mrs. Tammy
Pomeroy
Christie Bland
Jeffrey Brown
Joshua Brown
Kyle Chrestman

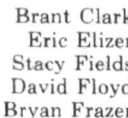

Brant Clark
Eric Elizer
Stacy Fields
David Floyd
Bryan Frazer

Craig Garrett
Johnny Garrett*
Ashley Gore
Narey Graves
Rachael Hampton

NO
PHOTO
AVAILABLE

Josh Jackson
Jason Judkins
Steve Moore
Lee Payne
Mary Rippy

Wayne Robinson
John Rose
Calvin Shofner*
Nicole Stites
Brittney Swindle

NO
PHOTO
AVAILABLE

Jessi Waugh
Missy White
Bryan York
Brent Young

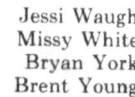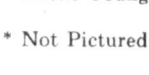

* Not Pictured

20

MRS. ROGAN'S FIRST GRADE

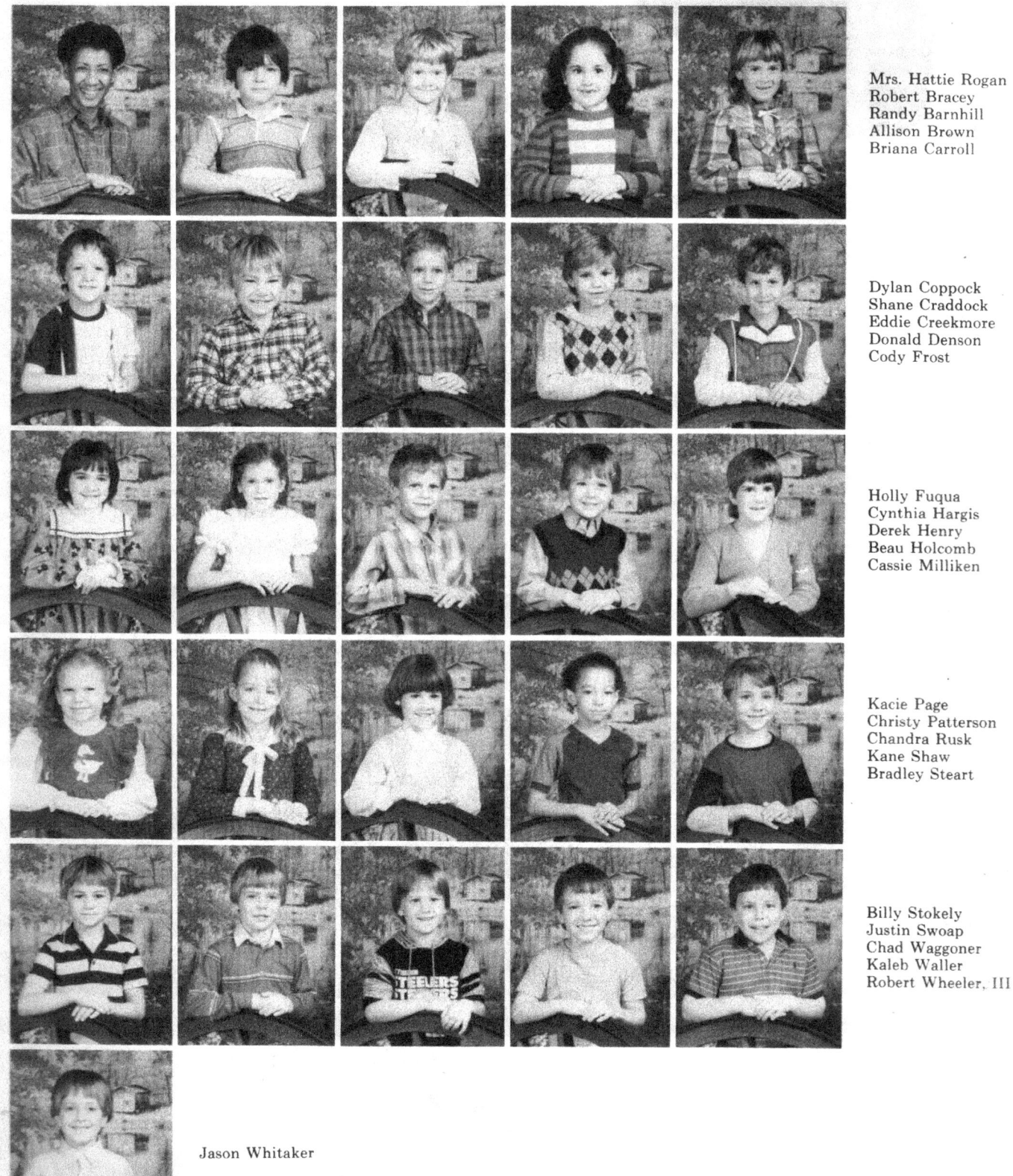

Mrs. Hattie Rogan
Robert Bracey
Randy Barnhill
Allison Brown
Briana Carroll

Dylan Coppock
Shane Craddock
Eddie Creekmore
Donald Denson
Cody Frost

Holly Fuqua
Cynthia Hargis
Derek Henry
Beau Holcomb
Cassie Milliken

Kacie Page
Christy Patterson
Chandra Rusk
Kane Shaw
Bradley Steart

Billy Stokely
Justin Swoap
Chad Waggoner
Kaleb Waller
Robert Wheeler, III

Jason Whitaker

Latini Amons
Roger Angell
Jordon Baker
Daniel Beavers
Christina Bozarth

Nathan Carlton
Shawn Dancer
Brandy Denson
Misty Douglas
Rachel Etter*

NO
PHOTO
AVAILABLE

Kelly Frakes
Ryan Hall
Mrs. Ellen Brown

Eric Martin*
Rachel Martin

NO
PHOTO
AVAILABLE

Paul Michael
McClellan
Andie Lee McRae
April Midgette
J.C. Oakley
Kristen Sargent

Jimmie Shafner
Rye Taylor
Andy Willis

* Not Pictured

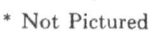 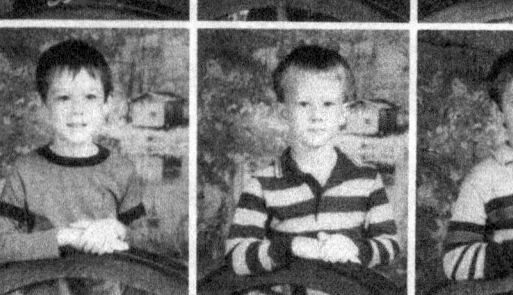

MISS BRUCE'S KINDERGARTEN

Tabitha Adams
Joey Bromley*
Paula Clark
Shannon Coleman
Jonathan Colvin

Rachel Cornelison
Eric Eim
Twyla Floyd
Brooks Hackett
Stephen Howell

Nicholas Huff
Bo Jackson
Miss Jamie Bruce

Kris Leggett
Lisa McBroom

Brent McGuire
Bobby Minick
Brandon Montgomery
Chrissi Smith
Lucas Smith

Chris Spencer*
Charlie Todd
Latasha Wright*
Amy Young

* Not Pictured

MRS. SHAW'S KINDERGARTEN

Joey Brinkley
Lee Camplin*
Gary Daniels*
Casey Davis
Ashley Douglas

NO
PHOTO
AVAILABLE

NO
PHOTO
AVAILABLE

Ryan Fey*
Beth Garrison
Sidney Hurst
Sharon Jakes
Latisha Jones

NO
PHOTO
AVAILABLE

Jamye McMurtry
Tim Milkwick
Mrs. Teresa Shaw

Alice Ragland
Wesley Rigsby

John Roberts
David Slate
Micha Smith
Kristen Swint
Ben Trotter

Kyle Waller
Johnathan West
Jordon Williams

* Not Pictured

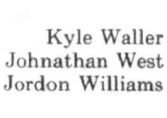